A POET'S HAGGADAH

PASSOVER THROUGH THE EYES OF POETS

EDITED BY RICK LUPERT

A POET'S HAGGADAH

Ain't Got No Press

Design and Layout ~ Rick Lupert
Cover Photo "Wine at Sunset" by Emo Saloy, Turkey

Thanks to Beyond Baroque, Richard Modiano, Fred Dewey, Annette Geis
Addie and Moses.

(818) 904-1021

or

15522 Stagg Street, Van Nuys, CA 91406

or

info@PoetSeder.com

or

www.PoetSeder.com

First Edition ~ First Printing ~ April, 2008

Printed by InstantPublisher.com
United States of America

ISBN: 978-0-9727555-8-0 $12.00

ORDER OF THE SEDER

"Wine is bottled poetry."

Robert Louis Stevenson

KADEISH

קדש

Manischewitz Moon   by Peggy Landsman

At the center of the table, Elijah's place is set.
He is served along with us although his food will not be touched.
His wine, however, seems to swell within the circle of its cup.

I look out the window.

Clouds slip silkily over the moon.
They're in the mood to play matzo cover,
Mistaking for matzo that old two-faced stone.

Who is young? Who wants money?

O, matzo-ball moon, roll your pesadiche light on over to me.
I long to see you shine in my Elijah's naked eyes.
I've always been a sucker for love at first sight.

And why should this night be different?

On this night, my sweet one, I swan-dive like syrup
Deep into dangerous cups.
I open all doors--not wisely, but wide.

On this night, I forget to be wary.

The haze around the paschal moon is red.
Some drunk must have dunked the Afikoman.

On this night, I find I've been chosen.

"All is in the hands of man.

Therefore wash them often."

Stanislaw J. Lec

RACHATZ

רחץ

The Importance of Hand Washing

by Leslie Halpern

He held my fingers in his hand
and gazed upon each digit
with such a keen intensity
that I began to fidget.

"How do you keep your nails so clean?"
He asked, dirty chin rubbing.
"I take a shower every day,
so my nails need little scrubbing."

Suddenly his face turned red
ablaze from cheek to cheek.
"I take two on certain days
so I can skip a few each week."

I found his bathing schedule
exceptionally funny.
He thought that you could save them up
like piles of unspent money

I said to him, "Suppose one day
you decide you'd like to splurge
and take seven showers in one day
to sate your weekly urge."

The bathing-impaired fellow
did not share my sense of glee,
for that dirty middle finger
was extended straight at me

13

"Joys divided are increased."

Josiah Gilbert Holland quotes

ＹACHATZ

Passover   by Robert Klein Engler

The window is open and I hear birds call.
I would bring him here on feathers, too.
Tell me, why is the word for "flame"
and "sharp edge of a sword" the same?
Broken matzoth has a new name.
So does a broken man.

"When I was very young, I was already a fabulador. I loved to give my own version of stories that everybody already knew. When I got out of a movie with my sisters, I retold them the whole story. In general they liked my version better than the one they had seen."

Pedro Almodovar

MAGGID

he Four Questions by Ellyn Maybe

honor the coming of Passover, I asked my mind to partake of a Seder.
t the table.

eavened anxiety flowed from the kitchen like a magician's endless scarf.
er herbs made onions of my eyes

re are 4 questions I'd like to ask but I'll settle for this one.
you love me?

dler on the Roof and its longing for a match, a miracle
a musical shtetl.

re is a place in our past that is less than a century old.
set a place at the table for it.

netimes it looks like 6 million hands reaching out for a bar of soap.
netimes it looks like a voter registration card sticking out of a swamp,
pped on the fingertips of Schwerner, Chaney and Goodman.
netimes it looks like the 5 year old face put on the post office wall
he taunts of Christ killer drown out any realistic chance for nap time.

ve a questioning nature.
es of how come surround me and tell me their bark is sweeter than
bite history has in mind for those swallowing the
colate coated T.V. sets.

4 question marks wearing the masks of horsemen
their hooves on the table like they own the place.
k for someone to hide the afikomin
nobody wants their hands to touch it.
he say I'm searching for a wish so powerful that the piece of matzoh
overed in a controversy of ash.

There's a cantor swaying in the Talmud, singing *next year in serenity*.
At first it sounds like a hummingbird doing pushups on the oracle of your
After 10 minutes, it sounds like the fire Kafka wanted to death his words in

There is a place at the table for Elijah.
Many glasses brim with L'Chaim to welcome the invisible world.
A family sits shivering for a week, trying to make forgiveness a verb.

I change the question from *do you love* me to *I love you*
There is matzoh on your breath.
I wonder, have you been searching for me too?

The Two Questions   by Adam Shechter

The Two Questions:

Why are all other nights usually the same as this one?

Because he is castrated and she is everywhere.

And it is from his suffering that I learned how to suffer, and she is what made my body, so like him I look with pathetic gaze. I must answer for all

Because he is angry and she is disappointed. They enjoy.

And I knew that I could do nothing, as my flesh was unleavened and loose, so I wandered within their house and got so far as an absence of all nourishment allows. And I ate upon my own analysis, voraciously imagining, and knew that I found the beginning of what it means to leave in every direction, but I was nowhere, and soon returned home, yet I was already there.

Because he is dying, and she is depressed. They enjoy.

So, they needed me and I returned. I saw that the house of my birth is everything. That my only body is this home. Though now feeding on the imperceptible movement of stale air, as my mother once fed me when I was inside her, as she continued to feed me at her nipple after I was born, with a soft melody of dust. Did I tell you there was no food?

Because she sees all this, and he knows. They enjoy.

And I felt the hunger begin with the hollow tickling, I gagged, at first quite small, the first ripple initiated in slender esophagus. Then the hours extinguished all cells, my body awoke in great agitation and the tickles filled thoughtlessly, first two scratches, then three, four, seven, ten, then forty. Forty fingers pelted the surface of my inflated abdomen sack. I heard crying. It was just me.

Because she sees all this, and he knows. They enjoy.

So the hunger was huge and took all of my body as a baby into the mouth of a giant sadist's lips. The sadist's mouth was also the baby's and the baby bit down on all of his body and his body was now gone. But he was all alone and soon realized that he was still hungry.

Because she sees all this, and he knows. They enjoy.

So, we know that this is all that there was. The baby biting onto the nothingness and the hunger soon returning. And when this toothless cutting and the return of empty ache crossed in cycle, then the baby knew a vibration from the deepest within.

Because she sees all this, and he knows. They enjoy.

A scream not meant for human ears.
The body shook to a violent pause.

Because she sees all this, and he knows. They enjoy.
And the baby understood what was to be his life.
As from within the orb where mind would soon be, there
        came a first vision
of a large smooth milk scented dome.
And the baby cried, screamed and wailed.
Because she sees all this, and he knows. They enjoy.
As the soft curving dome grew a small pink face,
A knotted nose appeared at its tippy-top.
And the baby howled the most abhorrent glorious shriek,

Ate and ceased complaint

But as an outside observer might notice, the baby's tightly puckered lips were chugging away at what was just air.

What constitutes a new night?

The Passover Offering. The opportunity to be passed over. To be spared suffering. To dodge the depressing transparent inheritance. The Passover offering sates misery's hunger, quiets the ancestral starvation. We feed the parental ghosts, feed them, freeze, free, intoxicate them with bread-flesh so they will float over us. Their anguish extinguished, murderous mechanical eyes, alive or already dead, are shut down with drunken yeast-less sleeping. Their selfish childish jaws have moved and it was not with the ligaments of our filial happiness coming apart in their stone teeth. We feed the past so we do not have to live in it. Be swallowed in it. Die in it. The past which curls up large and deserted, a bland white formation over everything. We eat mother's bitter shadows, move our lips with the glue that bound father's gloom, taste their hopeless familial oil on our tongues. We do not spit, choke, gag. Our mouths can think because they are with a new third parent. So we chew, tearing apart their narrow eternal structures. And at the core of this depressive carbohydrate is the tertiary joke, the Jewish community. Speak the traditional words and then leave Egypt. Down our throats, into our stomachs, and then out! We leave Egypt. Together, the family cataclysm is neatly organized around a table of suffering. A table symmetrically spread with cunning submission. A table passed over. We place ourselves in this friendly mannerism so as not to taste mom's desolation in our lives, but emerge out of a portal, the body memory of thousands of years made accessible in a simple ritual. Echoing, we taste the flat levity, impervious to our own appetite for famine, pouring, swishing with the filament of our starvation myth. We sit, happy time travelers grasping strangely neutered bread, crunching, still here, devouring the end of a long family night.

Kashas by Lynne Bronstein

Why is this night
different from all other nights?

Because tonight
even the kids get to drink wine
that's sweeter than Kool-Aid.
And after a while
The archaic grammar of the text
will be difficult to read
without a lot of giggles.

Because tonight
we will try to recline
and will mostly slip off our chairs
from the second hand pillows Mom padded them with.

Because tonight the special
silver plated service is out
and the cups with turquoise enameling
from Israel
that we usually just look at
through the glass windows of the cabinet.

Because tonight
the diet
goes out the window.

Because tonight
my mother will forget
that she said she could not sing

and by a miracle she will sing along
with Dyanu and Who knows One.
And my friend will observe
that he never saw my mother
so happy as when she sang at Passover.

Because tonight
my cousin will cover her ear
and complain of our irreverent sound effects
during Chad Gadya
the tale of the goat.
But it's what we've always done
for my father told us
of his father and uncles dancing on top of the table.
On Passover, we can be joyous
and we can be what might be called
irreverent

Because tonight Bob for once
may not have to read the part of the simple son.
Because tonight there is someone really young
who will read the four Kashes instead of my brother
who has been doing it into the years of gray.

Because tonight
The family feuds are suspended.
Because tonight we prove our valor
when the horseradish for moror, the bitter herb
goes up our noses.

Because tonight there is no TV
because we are the stars
and we don't exist in the work world the school world
the city world or the world world.
We exist only in our exodus world.
Our red sea crossing over
our ten plague surviving
our daily problem overcoming
worldly crisis triumphing
world,
kicking back our shoes under the table
as we laugh off the 3000 years since this journey
our most wonderful time of the year in the spring Holiday.
Because tonight is our night. And we rule.

Passover Blues   by Pam Ward

I don't know about you
But I got runaway slave roots
Roof jumpin' fools
Who'd rather rot
than be tied
who'd rather leap
than be horse whipped
or forced to work free
Who ran off, escaping
the torture & rape,
or being strung
like some clothes
on the line.

I don't know 'bout ya'll
But my grandma was slick
The original midnight creep,
she tipped off one moon.
Jumping two stories
all she took
from slavery's jaw
was a fat busted lip
& the almighty gall
Ducking through fields
hiking in hills
living on snake juice & grits
and "damn it, bitch
why won't you die?"
Wandering alone
just like Moses

for 40 long nights
until she hit
California's bent spine.

I don't know about yours
but I have blue overseer eyes
and the bondage still taints
the hue of my skin.
But I got grandma
black & rich
heatin' my neckbones & thighs
It's a renegade mix,
of pure spitfire & pride.
I won't pass-over
like some those
poor lost black souls.
I will flow, red & rich
like a good Seder wine.
Racing like the Pacific
whipping rock into slush.
Always running.
Always coming.
Each wave thunderous
& free
with the strength
of a run-away slave.

The First Seder by Diana Sher

On the morning
Before the first seder
I begin the accounting
The sky is clear blue
Empty
And I have given up
Almost everything
We will be alone tonight
Facing squarely
All that will never be
In the background
I hear a fragile melody
Celebrating
I have left Egypt.

Avadim Hayinu   by Beth Kanter

Remember. Once,

we were free.

Free women and men who crossed a sea,

walked thirsty and hot through a desert

to free.

But today,

we are slaves.

Enslaved to our own hearts hardened

by trans fatty acids and overexposure to reality TV.

Slaves to frequent flier miles, to online shopping and to

       pretending we don't read People magazine

to Ziploc bags, Diet Coke and to checking our email

       while sitting in the audience of preschool performances.

But remember. Once,

a long time ago,

we were free.

Free without credit card debt, the CNN crawl and ring tones.

Free without Prozac, Splenda and a war we hate but don't actively

protest.

Remember. Once,

a long time ago

we were slaves

but then

hot and hungry

we walked

free.

In The Midst of Flight They Forget
(Why *Prince of Egypt* Disappointed)

Parting

       seas! Evil

              swarms! Black

                     plagues!

Oh yes!

 It's a musical

Moses played by Batman.
(It's the staff–chicks did the staff?)
Catwoman appears to quote
the Kama Sutra.
The third row man notes:

"Ghandi didn't write the Kama Sutra..."

 Oceans migrate! Tides shift! The burning bush speaks
                                Ebonics!

When will you believe?

First born are taken-thrown
into car commercials, product placement. The Hollywood
sign is butchered, passed out to the drowning

33

masses. Mount Arrarat is auctioned off
in parcels on the Net. The winds of change whisper:
                              "Mariah..."

Oh, sweet Mariah!
Gives us her all!
Gives us a climax
every time!

Gives us Hollywood!
(As produced by Vegas.) Bubble gum
culture Manna cascades from Saffron painted skies.
(But it's $7.50 a pop
 and doesn't include parking.)

We stand dripping
in lambs blood as corporate spirits pass
above advertising the latest in teenage
footware. We raise strangled hands. Shout
hoarsely to broken nosed Gods:

                    "LET MY PEOPLE GO! "

                    "KLATU-BARATA-NICTO!"

                    "NIKE. JUST DO IT."

Hey, we are promised
some lovely violence: the head of Cole Porter.
His thin, piano fingers kicking and screaming

from a sampling board! The Gershwins fed
to the MGM lion! Over the Rainbow recast

in a woman's prison,
a girl's locker room,
a mud pit with two chesty strippers glinting
like beached, miracle fish in Galilee.

Hollywood is ready
for its close up. Demands disco, funk, Busby Berkely tricked
up in trip-hop

Oh, save a prayer
for the lizard tongued acolytes sacrificing sun flower faced ingenues
to Backstreet Boy's demographic!

Save a prayer for the machines grinding
our breath.

Save a prayer for the common
denominator. The trivial
pursuit.

The romantically tragic spreading
honeyed palms. Singing: *Hossana! Hossana in the highest!*

Shifra Talk to Her Friend Puah

by Julia Stein

Where do my words come from? It's a mystery.
When the Egyptian soldiers bound us and dumped us

in the throne room I was mute, just heard Pharaoh's
voice thunder an order to us to kill Hebrew boy babies.

At the next birth I held the male baby in my hand.
When he cried, you looked at him so terrified.

The words jumped out of my mouth: "We'll hide
him and his mother in the cave near Goshen."

The soldiers came again, tied us with chains.
In the palace they made our faces lick the floor.

Pharaoh said in icicle tones, "Why have you let
the male children live?" His words froze my bones.

For the first time I raised my head, stared at
an old man, wizened and ugly in a purple shroud.

My words swelled up: "The women hide and give
birth before we come." Pharaoh waved us away.

Puah, I never knew where my words come from;
only I must obey them. Now let's watch the Hebrews

put on the roof of the two stone houses they build for us,
houses sweet as dates, sturdy as the pyramids.

You Are Moses   by Richard Schiffman

Be not be depected, for the blossom
is sharp and silken. And patient, bearing the slushy mass,
bowed yet unbroken. And modest, shirking the limelight, hunched
like a mole in its clammy tunnel. Blind, but scrappy-- tougher
than the snow, more determined. And, yes, short-lived,
gone in a week, at most two, but don't forget,
the crocus

is only the first float in the parade.
More will follow. You will follow. That is what I am trying
to tell you. You, who are crushed and craven, you who bear so great
a weight upon you. And who are invisible even to yourself. You
too will rise, the blade of your waxen leaves, your velveteen blue
kimono, moist and pleated as the wings of a moth
not yet fled its cocoon.

You too will rise up from under the snow
of your own life. It has been such a long winter, and it is not yet over,
and you are tired, and the earth is tired, and the sodden blanket
lingers on besmirched and trampled, and the forecast is iffy,
for the next few weeks it could go either way. And you
can't be sure if flowering now is wise. There are
no guarantees that you will ever taste

the sun's kiss on your quilted lips.
And the beauty of it is-- it doesn't matter.
Whether you think that you are ready or not, and even
if there is a late blizzard, it doesn't matter. You are coming up
anyway, you were made for this and you will do it, you are
already doing it under the snow where even you
can't see what's happening

something is stirring. Do you feel it?
It doesn't matter-- the snow feels it, even if you don't.
Whether you have faith in my words, whether you have faith in yourself
is irrelevant, the snow is parting like the Red Sea. So what if Pharaoh
doesn't see it? Moses sees it. He is telling you to walk. You are
walking. He is telling you to unfurl in the dank darkness
your fragile petals,

but only the snow is truly fragile.
Though it looks like it will last, it won't-- but you will.
That is what I am trying to tell you. Your blossom will soon enough
be dust. It was not made to endure. But you are not those petals.
You are the ardor that pushes. Under the still frozen
soil of your own life something pushes.
You are that

irrepressible force which comes back
year after year-- a green spear, a blue fuse concealed
under the snow, under the stubborn stuckness of matter.
And you will not give up anytime soon. Mark my words, you will die
a thousand deaths, but you will not stop, because you are Moses,
and the Red Sea is parting, and someone-- it is not clear
who-- is beckoning,, beckoning
from the far shore.

Greatness   by S. Thomas Summers

It's not unusual to spy a toad
squat beneath the dogwood
as one squats now, legs coiled
beneath its rump, eyes placid
as puddles, yet camouflaging
deep concern. An expanse

of lawn and cedar chips stretch
between it and a tangle of ivy,
a sanctuary of shade beneath
the frayed hammock. Moses
must have felt this way, bellied
up to that sea, Rameses making
close behind – a pharaoh's desire
to devour a troublesome Jew.

Perhaps, this toad is praying,
calling to some amphibious lord
who will part the grass, divine
safe pass through unknown
spires of rye and Kentucky blue.

It waits – and then, without word
or croak, this prophet of warts
pops into the hands of fate,
of god, of grass – and again is still,
humped near hills of hidden ant colonies,
channels of twisting salamanders, where

it prays and listens for word or sign
to bound once more as a garter slicks under
the fence, slips its tongue, tastes an air
tainted with the spice of faithful reverence.

The Wicked Son   by Howard Camner

The Wicked Son counts himself out
It's not *his* scene, it's yours
He didn't make this world
It's not his problem
So he keeps to himself
He keeps constant
He watches from behind his walls
and never lifts a finger
except maybe to point or push or punish
The Wicked Son is bad news
He is self-contained, self-indulgent, and self-centered
He is a self-made mistake and he knows it
He don't care when you left, if you left, or where you went
He just wants to know why
The Wicked Son needs no one
He makes that loud and clear
with every move he makes
He spells it out for you
whether you need him to or not
He is a missing piece who never tried to fit it,
a black hole in the sky where a star should be,
and a creation all his own
The Wicked Son counts himself out
It's not his scene, it's yours

Upon Your House by Claudia Handler

I swear by the gall that swells in me,
I know you. I'll come after you.
Your instruments will not hold their tuning,
and your salt will ruin meat

A legacy of cross-eyed children,
who cannot smile and cannot think,
will fill you with a sizzling grief,
so that you can't unclench your throat.

And when your pillow greets your cheek,
words will swarm around your ears
that perfectly express your rage,
each point a chime, so deftly made,
nocturnal tongues that won't relent.

Just wait until you witness
this newfangled hail I've been working on,
and souped-up locusts that fly at you
like fists, despite their ample heft.
It only takes one to fill a mouth.

And all of this will leave your veins
so wrung, so pitted, and so pocked,
that they won't even plump
the slew of fleas I send to feast on them.

I'll bring exquisite flakes of venom
that I will blizzard in your blood.
I'll drag the choicest slabs of darkness
to batter down your door and roof.

And no, you can't disguise yourself,
your daughters, or your sons from me.
You can't outrun or outsmart me.
You can't hold your breath long enough.
I will protect who I want to protect.

And even now, out on the street,
The razor blades in your walls start to sing.
I see the teeth marks on your roses.
This must be the house.
This must be the house.

Blood, Frogs by Daniel Olivas

Blood, Frogs....
Do you know me, Adonai?
A latecomer to your Seder table?
A visitor waiting for Elijah?

Vermin, Wild Beasts....
You blessed the Moabite,
Ruth, with an honored place
in *Ketuvim*, so there must be
hope for me.

Pestilence, Boils....
My people have suffered, too,
though nothing like the Inquisition
or the Holocaust. But the Aztecs
were fooled and then slaughtered,
raped and oppressed by
the Spaniards who rode proud horses
roughshod over meso-America
creating a mixed *gente*,
the *Mestizos*. And then discrimination,
a glass ceiling we hit, in the great
country, as we scratch towards
the American dream.

Hail, Locusts....
But here I sit, a Jew for only
twelve years, looking at the
matzo, bitter herbs, shank bone,
amidst other symbols of oppression
and subsequent Exodus, Diaspora.

My wife's family (and even my son!)
easy and familiar with it all, as much
a second nature as my *Chicanismo*
is to me. But each year, I
recognize more and more,
mouthing the Hebrew faster and
faster. Is there hope for this old dog?

Darkness, Slaying of the First Born....
I took the name of Ysrael when
I converted because Jacob wrestled
with the angel and saw the face
of G-d, before he, too, became a
Jew and took a new name.
I wrestled, struggled (did I see
the face of G-d, too?), for over
six years before making the choice.
It is a choice I do not regret, but, at times,
when my ten-year-old son breezes through
the Four Questions in Hebrew (not English!),
I am a stranger searching in bewilderment's
twilight for my soul. Can an outsider
take on another people's traditions,
burdens and history while maintaining
his own proud history?
Can an outsider ever stop wandering?
Will I ever be at home?

Ten Plagues by Daniel Y. Harris

Blood

Cryptomyth of albumin
in the fishy
Nile—

the sorcerer burns
above stalks
of reed—

the red reach
stinks to high
stench—

blood gives
no conceit.

Coagula—

the theogonic
trick.

Frogs

Stretch your staff
to green
anura—

conjure eaters
of gastropods—

45

Aaron's horde—

Egypt
of copy
concedes—

the spell comes
and stays
to slime.

Lice

Strike at the dust,
this mass
of lice—

flip the finger
of God—

louse,
phthiraptera,
obligate

host—

clings to hair,
feeds on skin,
eggs laid

in the darkest dark
without rid.

Beasts

Swarm of mixture,
not in Goshen—

pangolins,
wildebeests,
wild bores,
hyenas—

worship
in the wilderness

miscreant
Moses,

and remove
the kill—

we starve.
No affection.

Pestilence

The death of horses,
donkeys, camels, cattle,
sheep and goats—

Israelite defense—

immune
this epizootic,

47

ulcerative
and arid—

drills to bone
the ride,
the source of food.

Boils

Handful of soot
skyward
to Pharaoh

festers to boil
on men
and livestock—

furuncle
of pus
and dead tissue

strike priests,
who once
in books

of the dead
healed
this eczema
of wind—

nobody

in bodies.

Hail

Hail mixed with fire—
preternatural
to orchards

and crops,
strained

to water ice,
cumulonimbus—

updrafts
in rare sand,
this time sin—

world-mastery
in prayer,

lands on no ground.
To disappear
without

promise.

Locusts

Harden the heart
and split

the sea—

compromise
the locust-spin

of migratory
acrida

to purge the plant
and tree—

when done,
they say, leave
us here.

Darkness

Irises of nyctophobe's
dilate—

sun-hunted
to bargain for three
days—

Horus is blind.
Zero rest
mass

of unnatural
black.

What God riots

eyes?

Take it.

Death of Firstborn

Submit and stroll
by the black
mould

of firstborns,
cladosporium—

the blooded
doorpost—

mark of marks,
tolls the bloodline
with algor
mortis—

no stutter
for a slavery
of arms.

Miriam's Song   by Julia Stein

I swept the house clean through nine plagues,
swept when Moses turned the river into blood,

swatted at frogs all day in the Egyptians' kitchen,
chased frogs in the bedrooms, whacked at them

on the beds, jumped after frogs in the kitchen. Next
I cleaned off lice from the heads of the Egyptians.

When my brother sent flies, the Egyptians had me
stand over their meals and beds swatting at flies.

After the Lord killed their cows, we laughed
even as we smelled that horrible stench.

Then I spent hours wrapping up the boils
all over the Egyptians' skin rejoicing.

The Egyptians made us women go into the fields,
round up their cattle, drive them into barns,

lock the doors against the pounding hail.
The day the locusts devoured the plants

I swept my home for house and swept three days that
the Egyptians sat in darkness, for only we had light.

Before the tenth plague I swept once more,
then roasted lamb and cut up bitter herbs we ate

remembering four hundred years of slavery
that terrible night the Angel of Death screeched

and screamed as he flew over our houses
on his bloody way to kill the Egyptians' sons.

We were leaving so I baked my bread unleavened,
packed clay crockery, black pots onto a rickety cart.

I wanted to smash the pyramids.
We'd built them well. They'd last. A pity.

At the Red Sea, after we climbed onto the land and
saw Pharaoh lead his chariots into a gap

riding between two huge cliffs of water when
mountains of water crashed down on them,

I called the women who came with cymbals and drums,
"Come dance now for we are flying into freedom."

Haiku for Pass-over by Michael Levy

Teaching at the Seder table
God's loving kindness
killing first born

Dayenu   by Barbara Elovic

because my father wasn't passed over

If he could have kept his hands from shaking
Dayenu, it would have been enough.
If he could have outpaced a baby
crossing a room-- *Dayenu*.
If my grandmother hadn't shouted
at him when he landed on his back,
"Come on now, pick your feet off the ground,"
it would have been enough.
If my father hadn't locked my mother out
of the apartment and sounded the fire alarm
in the middle of the night
it would have been enough.
If he hadn't torn his ear
when he careened into the kitchen counter
staring at the blood as if it fell from the sky
it would have been enough.
If he could have blown sufficient air
from his mouth to make a sound
intelligible to other people
it would have been enough.
If he could have fed himself
or known what he was eating-- *Dayenu*.
If his sister hadn't decided
he was overmedicated
and flushed his pills down the toilet it would have been enough.
If his brother hadn't refused
to help with the medical bills
because I was a bad granddaughter
it would have been enough.

55

If my mother hadn't boarded him
in the nursing home the last eight months
it would have been enough.
If his brother hadn't thrown a fit
at the home on his one visit
claiming my father was too young to be there
it would have been enough.
If his brother had visited more than once
in five years it would have been enough.
If my grandmother hadn't told me she never called
because talking to my father made her sad
it would have been enough. *Dayenu.*
If she had called once
it would have been enough.
If my father hadn't thrown the pillow at me
angry because I was healthy
Dayenu --it would have been enough.
If I could be sure he recognized me
the last time I visited
it wouldn't really have made a difference.
It couldn't have been enough.
Enough already.
Day-dayenu, dayenu, dayenu.

dayeinu by Rachel Kann

had you-i been given but seconds in this unreal reality,
and the ten-thousand things not made themselves known to me-you,
daiyenu,

had the ten-thousand things made themselves known to me-you,
and your-my blood not thudded circuitously, stubbornly,
daiyenu,

had your-my blood thudded circuitously, stubbornly,
and these atoms not stayed gathered into matter as me-you,
daiyenu,

had these atoms stayed gathered into matter as me-you,
and you-i not been born earthly entity,
daiyenu,

had you-i been born earthly entity,
and these lungs not breathed me-you,
daiyenu,

had these lungs breathed me-you,
and you-i not strengthened from struggling,
daiyenu,

had you-i strengthened from struggling,
and the time-space web not caught me-you,
daiyenu,

had the time-space web caught me-you,
and you-i not made manifest believed-in possibility,
daiyenu,

had you-i made manifest believed-in possibility,
and never felt faith inside me-you,
daiyenu,

had you-i felt faith inside me-you,
and not lost ego-identity,
daiyenu,

had you-i lost ego-identity,
and not detached from a conceptually separate me-you,
daiyenu,

had you-i detached from a conceptually separate me-you,
and never found inner tranquility,
daiyenu,

had you-i found inner tranquility,
and never let angel-death tongue-kiss me-you,
daiyenu,

had you-i let angel-death tongue-kiss me-you,
and not answered with reciprocity,
daiyenu,

had you-i answered with reciprocity,
and not still vibrated energy for eternity,
had you-i been given but seconds in this unreal reality,
had it all been arbitrary,
had it all been but a word,
a breath,
a blink,
a touch,
a grace,
a pulse,
a truth,
daiyenu,
daiyenu,

daiyenu.

Go Get Drunk And Take Your Place

G. David Schwartz

Go get drunk and take your place
Just down town and beside your face
Take a good look
At the postal book
And then just jump in the lake
Go get drunken up at the old house
And don't care just whose a souse
Take just one more gaze
Into the barmaids face
Then stamp the stamps on the letter

"Isn't there any other part of the matzo you can eat?"

Marilyn Monroe

MOTZI-MATZAH

מוֹצִיא-מַצָּה

Saying the Blessing Over Matzah

by Salvatore Buttaci

A God Who tends to our daily needs
created us out of dirt and dust,
not because He was lonely. He breathed
life into Adam and Eve for love's
sake, to share His world with humanity,
and despite the Eden betrayal,
His love remains undiminished.

In the desert He caused manna to rain
on the heads of the starving, the hopeless.
He sent angels to guide us in righteousness,
prophets to keep us rooted in our faith.

O Blessed are You, King of the Universe!
We have done so little to merit
Your boundless charity. This matzah we eat,
this Seder of remembrance, remind us
you are the Light of our existence.
Without You, we stumble in darkness.
Every breath, every word from our lips,
are prayers delivered to Your heavens!

Freedom From Egypt by Lanie Shanzyra P. Rebancos

open the window
let Elijah in
now we're free

trust tested
through hunger and
sea water

freedom from Egypt
after plague
rabbi took the bread

"Training is everything. The peach was once a bitter almond; cauliflower is nothing but cabbage with a college education."

Mark Twain

MAROR

מרור

Bitter by Heather McNaugher

This Passover, your Hebrew drones and treks its way to me.
Seder has me seated by your mother and your high school crush.
On either side, these mounds of precedent –
your source and sore spots of a quarter century.

Everybody here knows when to chant and tip the cup. I follow,
a murmur and a gulp behind. I try to fill your days
better than God.
Over sprigs and plagues your Hebrew blurts its place in my life.
Your eyes kindle backwards across a prayer.

Maror   by Jonathan Penton

Every night, I think of your betrayal
And the bitterness floods my bag
to form a heavy shelter
That protects me from my enemies
That warms me in dead desire

And every morning, I tear my shelter down
I think only of the warmth of your body
So that I might freeze in the desert sun
I carve your name into the flesh of murderers
To share with them the freshness of my wounds

"Worries go down better with soup."

Jewish Proverb

SHULCHAN ORECH

שלחן עורך

Not Sitting Shiva by Joan Pond

Jerry was whiter than I remembered, and his lips were taut.

I reached over to fix a lock of his hair,

then stopped.

I'd almost touched a corpse.

I sat beside him, smelling Bubby's brisket and potato kugel;

thinking of her applesauce and lemon cake.

Then, suddenly,

I started to shake inside.

I should be ashamed;

only thinking of myself.

But Jerry always liked food, the gathering of family, and close friends.

This was a time to make amends;

to bury the hatchet, along with the dead.

And as Bubby came from the kitchen with a platter

of chicken liver and bow ties,

I swear,

I almost saw

Jerry smile.

At Dinner by Elizabeth Iannaci

I'll bear the specter of some slaughtered
bird with its crepe-paper booties, nesting
in the middle of the table, it's crouton guts
spilling onto the pewter tray, bear the reports
from the plastic surgeon who finds half-eaten
sandwiches lost in the folds of fat while
he suctions off a small bit of a patient's
excesses, nod appropriately as the plaid-
bedecked sportsman holds forth
about the Thanksgiving he drew
a bead on the turkey that drowned while drinking
from a pond. Not the smartest bird,
(scientists have shown that the average Tom
will get sexually aroused merely by seeing
a rubber turkey-head mounted on a stick –
the avian equivalent of a supermodel) I will
endure another year of silly putty
melted into my velvet skirts,
yam-fisted toddlers' sticky-lipped whispers,
the lopsided strays and the severely relocated
who, drawn to my son's welcoming roost
make it a night unlike any other,
and I will be thankful for it all.

"Dessert is probably the most important stage of the meal, since it will be the last thing your guests remember before they pass out all over the table. "

William Powell

ZAFON

after Dan Savage   by Jonathan Penton

what knowledge
in this box of Doritos and religion
what is it you try to remember

having never tasted the infinite
why are you waiting
for eternity to resume?

"If you see no reason for giving thanks,

the fault lies in yourself."

Native American Proverb

BAREICH

Free by Devin Davis

unclean
ravens above ...

will be
a blessing ...

but, wouldn't you
rather us vacuum up?

come home,
walk on bogus rugs ...

at least the plates,
once rinsed by hand
—and set at this table,

where your own glass is
poured over half-full—
should have plenty ...

i am not sure
whether the door can remain open.

 ... perhaps we won't have enough
faith.

here, eat ...
what has been dead
for some time—& frozen
—let a good wife prepare ...

then drink. take
two bottles of wine.

from "Seder" by David Gershator

III

I go to the door to peek through the peephole:
it seems so daring to open the door for nothing
but if I open the door
I must be opening it for something
or maybe we're all crazy
inspired by a mad quest
for an answer in make believe

In back of me an aunt says
It might be smarter to open a window!
I stand by the door
The table is impatient:
No...I hear voices.
God help us, he hears voices!
No, really, I don't want people out there
to think I'm nosy. Let them pass.
I take another peek
Voices and footsteps
coming up the tenement stairs
An uncle calls: Anyone there?
A cousin answers: Not yet, not yet, but who knows
Shush, someone shushes
Is this the Last Supper or a quiz show?
Come on, let's go--

Visitation   by Larry Colker

It seemed as farfetched
for Elijah to visit every seder
and drink from every cup
as for Santa Claus
to visit all those homes
and eat all those cookies

and yet

opening the door
is such a steadfast gesture,
a silver cup of sweet, purple wine
is such heartfelt offering

I believed only a god
soured on humankind
could refuse
to bless us.

We never saw Elijah
but blessings arrived.

"What hymns are sung.

What praises said.

For homemade miracles of bread?"

Louis Untermeyer

HALLEL

הלל

Praise Small Things by Judith Pacht

Red clay tradebeads in a dreadlock braid,
the scent of earth-musk after rain,
a cicada chorale shrieking in the sun,
the summer's chalky grass, oak-black shade.
Praise the sticky pollen on the bee's
hind legs, the blossom's private parts, the fruit.
Praise all vowels: masa and metate,
smooth and avocado,   quesadilla.
Praise Nomo backing first base on Beltre's throw,
Cohen reaching Ahmed, Ahmed reaching
words both used to know, speaking, speaking.
Praise the wild geese rising slow,
circling after rain to taste the scent
of air, of earth, this earth.

Enosh Introduces Idolatry

by Scott Alixander Sonders

"Then to call in the name of God became profaned."
Genesis, 4:26

God is dead!
Gott ist dead! I heard
every argument
but nothing
was said.

And when at last
they quit
the game
their name in stone, alone
remained.

And so, I know
as I survive,
god is – alive.
god is – alive.

"If I forget thee, O Jerusalem, let my right hand wither, let my tongue cleave to my palate if I do not remember you, if I do not set Jerusalem above my highest joy."

Psalm 137:5-7

NIRTZAH

Just Like Brian Wilson by Marc Jampole

Do not believe in kings.
When others sing, In Jerusalem next year,
shunning David's city, chant instead
Wherever you want to be:
in Paris or another European hub
studying the texture of paint under glass,
in the dust behind the plate, mask on,
in movement eyes closed swinging free
above the games and funnel cake,
swatting back half-budded branches in the sound of boots slogging,
well-oiled, feet in sand, adrift in a book of lust,
or behind the closed door of a small room
overlooking a large view of the world
well-lit walls cluttered with fragments
hunched on a slightly hard chair
by the tools you need to think about things.

Also a Full Moon by Helen Bar-Lev

Here in Spain
there is also a full moon
and the hotel
celebrates our exodus
from the holyland
five long days ago
with dishes of calamari
and other sea fruit delicacies;
flamenco dancing
is an after-dinner delight

The full moon and I
eye each other,
he chastises me –
what you doing here
when you should be home
in your Jerusalem
and not in Spanish exile –
don't you realize
how difficult it was
for the Lord to get you
out of Egypt,
that it was not easy
to move the earth
and the heavens,
to part waters,
and you in your gratitude
flee to Spain,
from which you were forced to exodus
five centuries ago,
from which your kin
were forbidden to return
by rabbinical proclamation,
and this whole land

screams it,
its history
repeats its stupidity
ad infinitum,
and to this country you come
for the convenience
of ignoring
the commemoration
of that other evil exodus
from Egypt
five centuries
plus three thousand
years ago,
before the fact of Christ
entered any
contemporary imagination,
before Queen Isabella
claimed Christ enticed her
to rape the Americas,
expel you Jews?

You know this,
every molecule of you senses it
it has entered your blood stream,
your collective Jewish memory,
it explodes your emotions,
pellets your conscience
and here you thought
you would find
a peaceful vacation,
in this nation alien?

Go home!
says the full moon,
soon,
I say,
soon...

"The present is the ever moving shadow that divides yesterday from tomorrow. In that lies hope."

Frank Lloyd Wright

Hayei Olam (Misheberach) by Jake Marmer

Misheberach, the post-blessing list of relatives,
he rattles them off like gunfire, a dozen
patrimonial shots, then the second cousins,
a battalion of great-aunts, friends,
neighbors, and their battalion of great-aunts,
heavily-breathing maiden names, fake passports,
pseudonyms, kinky monikers, repressed and
never translated pre-trans-atlantic identities,
dubs and doppelgangers, father-ghosts, gilgul-treetops,
alter-egos-separated-at-birth, nobel laureate stillborn pushing
further and further back, rowing millions
the peacock tail of the pie in which
we notice ourselves and begin shouting,
shouting, shouting like roosters and bears
and dancing with situps Ukrainian style
and the air is made out of Jewish names
it's the shaker-shuckling-sugared-god-grilled tornado –

that jumps inside the two-minute cup
of the gebbai's mouth

which closes

and the man steps back, to the side of the bimah.

Passover – In Loving Memory

by Misha Weidman

We are lighting the candles, Mutti. The table is set:
the roasted egg and broken shank,
the bitter herbs we dip in tears.
We will tell the story of redemption,
but you are not here.

Now, your veins are tubes through which the dark blood flows.
Your lungs are drowning, your arms bloated and bruised.
Yet, still your brow furrows when I bend to kiss your face.
Your hand trembles, neither letting go nor holding on.

Are you listening Mutti? Can you hear
the cartwheels on the cobble-stones,
the geese in the yard,
the great bells ringing out across the square?
Were those the days, Mutti, though you never said so,
when you ruled household and geschäft
with cool efficiency and thrift,
when you knew full well the figure you cut,
so elegant and so severe,
your dark hair up, your eyes burning,
poised, alone?

And when boots clattered in the town square and you shuttered up the sto
when you passed your daughter through the last train's window
and fled into the streets of Prague,
when Europe was burning and the gates were shut,
did you still think each day to braid your hair and pin it high, high up?

We are eating the bread of affliction, Mutti;
we are recounting the exodus.
So many dead! Six million and the ten or so
you called your friends -- do you hear them
above the roar of your own blood,
the gentle inrushing of your breath?

And if neither the sweatshops of New York
nor the palm trees of Los Angeles would yield their promise;
if, even with your fine new language
you peddled furs in a dingy department store,
and slept each night in a Murphy bed off Miracle Mile,
even then the neighbors bowed and let you pass;
the cousins in their mansions, the ones you'd cursed and fed,
seated you at their table and held their breath.

The door is closing and Elijah, if he has come at all, has gone.
The machine turns and a century of blood
is slowly cleansed of memory and pain.
In the end, you grew not to care so much.
The braided bun, your crown, was set aside.
Then the beauty parlor was too far.
My mother combed the wisps of hair away
while you complained about the maid.

The door is closing, Mutti.
Sleep. We are here with you.
Sleep. We will light the candles.

ABOUT THE CONTRIBUTORS

Helen Bar-Lev was born in New York in 1942, has lived in Israel for 37 years. She hold a BA in Anthropology. Since 1973 she has had over 80 exhibitions of her watercolour and pencil landscapes. Her poems and illustrations have been published in numerous internet and print anthologies. She and her partner Johnmichael Simon are the authors of *Cyclamens and Swords and Other Poems About the Land of Israel* (Ibbetson Press, Boston USA) in 2007. She is editor-in-chief of the *Voices Israel Annual Anthology* and a member of the Israel Artists' and Sculptors' Association.

Lynne Bronstein is the author of *Border Crossings, Thirsty In the Ocean,* and *Roughage* and has been published in P*oeticDiversity, Poetry Super Highway, Caffeine, On Target, Playgirl* and other magazines. She is a reporter for the *Santa Monica Mirror* and has written for numerous LA area newspapers and for cable TV news. Her short story "Why Me?" won First Runner Up in Poetic Diversity's Short Fiction contest in 2006.

Salvatore Buttaci has been writing poetry, fiction, and nonfiction since 1957. His first published piece that year was an essay, "Presidential Timber," in the *Sunday New York News* when he was sixteen years old. In December 2007, he was the recipient of the $500.00 *Taj Mahal Poetry Award.* After retiring from years of teaching, he and his wife recently moved from New Jersey to live in Princeton, West Virginia. "Writing everyday keeps me young, sane and happy. It rates a close second to the love of my life, Sharon."

Howard Camner is the author of 16 books of poetry. His works are housed in major literary collections worldwide. He received the first annual *MiPo Literary Award* in 2004 and was named "Best Poet of 2007" in the *Miami New Times* "Best of Miami" issue.

Larry Colker has co-hosted the Redondo Poets at Coffee Cartel weekly reading series for nine years. His limited-edition chapbooks are *What the Lizard Knows* (2003), and *Hunger Crossing* (with Danielle Grilli, 2006). In 2006 he was selected by Charles Harper Webb as the poetry winner of the Poets & Writers' California Poetry Exchange contest. He lives in San Pedro.

devin wayne davis has written well-over 2,000 poems. His publication credits include: the Sacramento Anthology: *100 poems, Sanskrit, Dwan, PDQ, Dandelion, Coe Review, Rattlesnake, Taproot, Chiron Review* and *39 chapbooks*. Selections can be sought on-line. davis has read as a featured poet at major book retailers. davis has written for Sacramento, CA. arts & entertainment weeklies, and worked for UPS and the State of California. davis served in the U.S. Army. He visited Spain, Germany, Switzerland, France, and was last assigned to Ft. Bragg, N.C.. as a photojournalist. davis earned a Bachelors degree in Journalism and History. davis has three daughters.

Barbara Elovic has published in more than 100 journals anthologies including *Poetry, Marlboro Review and Walk on the Wild Side: Urban American Poetry Since 1975* (Scribners) and *I Speak of the City: Poems of New York* (Columbia University Press). She published 2 chapbooks and is also one of the founding editors of the New York-based poetry journal, *Heliotrope* She lives in Brooklyn, NY.

Robert Klein Engler lives in Oak Park, Illinois and sometimes New Orleans. Many of Robert's poems and stories are set in the Crescent City. "Red Beans and Rice," is online at the *Drunken Boat*, and "The Approach to Pilottown," is at *Blithe House Quarterly*. His long poem, *The Accomplishment of Metaphor and the Necessity of Suffering*, set partially in New Orleans, is published by Headwaters Press, Medusa, New York, 2004. He has received an Illinois Arts Council award for his "Three Poems for Kabbalah." If you google his name, then you may find his work on the Internet. Some of his books are available at Lulu.com. Visit him on the web at RobertKleinEngler.com

David Gershator was born on Mt. Carmel too many years ago. Taught Humanities at Rutgers, Brooklyn College, CUNY, and the University of the Virgin Islands. Translations, poetry, and reviews in numerous anthologies and journals. Editor, *Downtown Poets Co-op* (1970's-80's). Associate Editor, *Home Planet News*. Recipient of NEH grant and NY State CAPS award. Translated and edited *Federico García Lorca: Selected Letters* (New Directions). Co-author of six picture books for children. Poetry books include *Play Mas'* and *Elijah's Child*. CD for children, Spring 2008: "This Is the Day: Storysongs and Singalongs." Works as printmaker and artist available on www.davidgershator.com

Leslie Halpern was a 13-year stringer for The Hollywood Reporter and is the author of the nonfiction books *Reel Romance: The Lovers' Guide to the 100 Best Date Movies, Dreams on Film,* and the upcoming

Passionate About Their Work: 150 Celebrities, Artists, and Experts on Creativity. A member of the performing troupe, *Poetry Ensemble of Orlando*, Leslie has published poetry in the award-winning anthology *Windows to the World*, *The Journal of Graduate Liberal Studies*, *True Romance Magazine*, *Scifaikuest*, *The Mother is Me*, and other publications.

Claudia Handler is a native New Yorker who has lived in Los Angeles for seven years. She has read at many L.A. venues, and appeared on several radio shows, including the popular public radio show, *Live Wire Radio*. Her poems have appeared in journals, as well as the online magazine, *Speechless*. Claudia was selected by Beyond Baroque to read in the Aloud Series at the Downtown Library. A co-director of Valley Contemporary Poets, she is also the author of *Going Under*. Claudia is the granddaughter of renowned poet Menke Katz, who wrote in both English and Yiddish.

Daniel Y. Harris is the author of the forthcoming poetry book, *Unio Mystica*. He is a widely published poet, essayist and visual artist. Among his credits are: *The Pedestal Magazine, Exquisite Corpse, In Posse Review, Mad Hatters' Review, Sein und Werden, Zeek, Poetry Salzburg Review, Wilderness House Literary Review, Poetry Magazine.com, Convergence* and *The Other Voices International Project*. Among his art exhibitions credits are: The Jewish Community Library of San Francisco, Market Street Gallery, The Euphrat Museum and The Center for Visual Arts. He earns his living as Northwest Regional Director of Development for Canine Companions for Independence. His website is www.danielyharris.com

Elizabeth Iannaci is a long-time Los Angeles resident who has appeared at countless U.S. venues as well as in Paris, Slovenia, and remote parts of Orange County. Recently awarded an MFA in Poetry from Vermont College of Fine Arts, she has one chapbook of poetry, *Passion's Casualties*, and her work has been widely published and anthologized. Iannaci served as a director of the Valley Contemporary Poets for five years, has one son and prefers paisley to polka dots.

Marc Jampole is the author of *Music from Words*, published in 2007 by Bellday Books, Inc. His poetry has been published in *Mississippi Review, Oxford Review, Janus Head, Main Street Rag, Ellipsis, Wilderness House Review* and other journals. Over the years, four of Marc's poems have been nominated for The Pushcart Prize. More than 450 articles he has written on various subjects have been published in magazines and newspapers.

Rachel Kann, winner of a James Kirkwood Award in fiction, LA Weekly Award and Backstage West Critic's Pick Garland Award, brings her work to stages as diverse as Disney Concert Hall, Royce Hall, and California Plaza in Los Angeles, The San Francisco Palace of Fine Arts, and the Vans Warped Tour, to name just a few. She also features at poetry landmarks like The Nuyorican Poets' Café, Beyond Baroque, and The Green Mill. Her poetry has appeared in various anthologies and journals, most recently *Word Warriors* from Seal Press. Rachel is currently completing her MFA in fiction.

Beth Kanter is a feature writer who has written about everything from the women of Afghanistan long before they were in the public eye to how to break up with your book club to her mother's bad cooking. Beth's work has appeared in dozens of magazines, newspapers and web sites including *Parents, American Baby, Working Mother, Shape, Wondertime, Fitness, the Chicago Tribune, Fodor's Washington DC 2008, the New York Jewish Week, the Washington Jewish Week* and *Pages*. Beth also holds an MSJ from Northwestern University.

Peggy Landsman's poetry and prose has been published in both online and print literary journals and anthologies, including *The Kerf, Thema, Spindle, Poetica, The Muse Strikes Back* (Story Line Press), *The Largeness the Small Is Capable Of* (Score Press), *Jewish Affairs,* and *Bridges* (Indiana University Press). Her first poetry chapbook, *To-wit To-woo*, is available from FootHills Publishing. You can visit her web site at http://home.att.net/~palandsman/

Michael Levy is an international radio host and is the author of eight inspirational books. Michael's poetry and essays now grace many web sites, newspapers, journals and magazines throughout the world. He is a prominent speaker on health maintenance, stress eradication, wealth development, authentic happiness and inspirational poetry. His new book, *The Inspiring Story of Little Goody Two Shoes*, is available at all good book stores and Michael's web site: http://www.pointoflife.com/

Jake Marmer is a NYC poet, and managing editor of the *Mima'amakim Journal of Jewish Art*. His current artistic efforts are tightly focused on Frantic Turtle, the punk-jazz-poetry band. More info on that: http://www.myspace.com/franticturtle

Ellyn Maybe is the author of *The Cowardice of Amnesia* (2.13.61), *Walking Barefoot in the Glassblowers Museum* (Manic D Press), *The Ellyn Maybe Coloring* Book (Sacred Beverage Press), and the following self-published books, *Putting My 2 Cents In* and *Praha and the Poet*

as well as the CD, *Ellyn Maybe Live.* She has been in many anthologies and has read throughout the country and internationally. www.ellynmaybe.com

Heather McNaugher is Assistant Professor of English in Chatham University's MFA program and poetry editor of *Fourth River.* Her chapbook, *Panic & Joy*, was recently published by Finishing Line Press. Her work has appeared in *Paper Street, The Bellevue Literary Review, Blithe House Quarterly, The Paterson Literary Review, Twelfth Street Review*, and *The Cortland Review.*

Daniel Olivas is the author of four books: *Devil Talk: Stories* (Bilingual Press, 2004); *Assumption and Other Stories* (Bilingual Press, 2003); *The Courtship of María Rivera Peña* (Silver Lake Publishing, 2000); and the children's book, *Benjamin and the Word* (Arte Público Press, 2005). Olivas is also the editor of *Latinos in Lotusland: An Anthology of Contemporary Southern California Literature* (Bilingual Press, 2008). His writing has appeared in the *Los Angeles Times, Jewish Journal, El Paso Times, Poetry Super Highway*, and many other publications. Website: www.danielolivas.com

Judith Pacht's manuscript was a finalist for the 2008 Philip Levine Prize, the Tupelo Press (2007-8) and the University of Arkansas open submission competitions. She won Honorable Mention in the 2007 Robert Frost Award competition, the 2007 Robinson Jeffers Tor House Prize for Poetry, and the Smartish Pace Erskine J. Poetry Prize. Pacht was first place winner in the Georgia Poetry Society, Edgar Bowers competition, and received the Margaret Reid High Distinction Award. Her work includes poems published in *Ploughshares; Runes, Arctos Press; Cider Press Review; The Los Angeles Review, Red Hen Press; Solo 6; Site of the City, Los Angeles postcard competitions;* and *Gastronomica*, The University of California Press.

Jaimes Palacio has been published all over the United States and Europe including, most notably, twice in *Art Life* and 3 major Tebot Bach anthologies. Most recently he was published in the Moon Tide Press anthology *Tidepools*. He has hosted several readings, had a column in *Next... Magazine*, created the New Voices showcase for The Orange County Poetry Festival and co-produced/hosted *I Am Not Dead Yet! A Derrick Brown Benefit*. He works for Fly By Night D.J.s and at the moment really needs jobs. http://www.bebo.com/peng88

Jonathan Penton has never been to war, but he did provide software support to G. Gordon Liddy. You can learn less about him at http://jonathan.unlikelystories.org/

Joan Pond lives in New Milford, Connecticut. She is the author of the book *A Rose Garden*. (Greystone Press)

Lanie Shanzyra P. Rebancos is a Filipino author of *On Our Way Home* and *Another Morning*. She is also a published poet and reviewer. Her works has been published and commented as well worldwide. Lanie is one of the associate editors of *Canadian Zen Haiku Journal*. She is currently working on her third anthology.

Richard Schiffman is a writer and journalist based in New York City. He has done reporting and commentary for National Public Radio. His spiritual writing includes two books, *Mother of All* published by Blue Dove Press, and *Sri Ramakrishna, A Prophet For the New Age*, published by Paragon House. He has just completed a third book on the mystical meaning of the Hebrew Exodus.

G. David Schwartz is the former president of Seedhouse, the online interfaith committee. Schwartz is the author of *A Jewish Appraisal of Dialogue*. Currently a volunteer at Drake Hospital in Cincinnati, Schwartz continues to write. His new book, *Midrash and Working Out Of The Book* is now in stores or can be ordered.

Adam Shechter is a writer and spoken word artist who was born, raised and continues to reside in Brooklyn, New York. He received his BA in literature from Hunter College and has studied extensively at the Mid-Manhattan Institute for Psychoanalysis. He is the editor of the online arts and culture journal, *The Blue Jew Yorker* found at www.bluejewyorker.com. His poetry has been published in *The Minnesota Review*, *Psychoanalytic Perspectives*, *Mima'amakim*, *Home Planet News* and *The Subway Chronicles*, among other publications. Adam has also performed his work in numerous venues around New York city.

Diana Sher teaches in the English department at Metropolitan State College of Denver. She is published in over eighty literary and commercial magazines including *Kalliope*, *Jewish Women's Literary Annual*, and *The New Delta Review*. Her chapbook, *After I Cut the Cord*, was released by Finishing Line Press in 2003.

Scott Alixander Sonders is the current President of California Writers - www.calwriterssfv.com - the oldest & largest organization of its kind. Although not raised religiously, on his own accord Scott matriculated two years in a notorious mystical Yeshiva in Jerusalem. He later garnered a Ph.D. in Literary Pedagogy, after completing his doctoral dissertation on "A Feminist Deconstruction of Genesis Text." Scott has +100 publication credits, was once nominated for a Pulitzer, and can be found on Amazon and in Barnes & Noble. He teaches Writing Workshops at Valley College.

Julia Stein has four books of poetry: *Under the ladder to Heaven, Desert Soldiers, Shulamith,* and *Walker Woman.* She has organized the panel *New California Literature: Breaking Into the Future* at the April 12 California Studies Association in Berkeley. She teaches at Santa Monica College.

S. Thomas Summers is a teacher of Writing and Literature at Wayne Hills High School in Wayne, NJ. He is the author of two poetry chapbooks: *Death Settled Well* (Shadows Ink Publications, 2006) and *Rather, It Should Shine* (Pudding House Press, 2007). Summers's poems have appeared in several literary journals and reviews: *The English Journal, MiPo, 2River View, The Pedestal Magazine, Words-Myth,* etc. Currently, Summers is completing a volume of American Civil War poetry - *Private Hercules McGee: Poems of the Civil War.* He lives in Northern New Jersey with his wife and children.

Pam Ward is a LA native, a writer and a graphic designer. A UCLA graduate and recipient of a 'California Arts Council Fellow in Literature' and 'New Letters Literary Award' she has had her poetry published in *Scream When you Burn, Grand Passion, Calyx, Catch the Fire* and has self published her own chapbook, entitled *Jacked-Up.* Her first novel, *Want Some, Get Some,* March 07, Kensington Press takes place after the blazing LA riots and her second novel, *Bad Girls Burn Slow,* Aug. 2008 is about the funeral business and identity crime. Pam has edited five anthologies including, *Picasso's Mistress, What the Body Remembers* and *The Supergirls Handbook: A Survival Guide featuring Los Angeles black female poets.* She has had short stories printed in *The Best American Erotica, Men We Cherish,* and *Gynomite.* Pam operates a graphic design studio and mentors at Art Center College of Design. Visit Pam at pamwardwriter.com

Misha Weidman wrote his first poem at age 9. He was born and raised in Sydney, Australia, where his Czech parents emigrated after World War II. Misha moved to Los Angeles in his teens, studied English Literature at U.C.L.A and received a law degree from Boalt Hall in Berkeley. He has continued to write poetry throughout a varied career in law, business, and real estate. His poems have been published online at *Melic Review.* He is also a published food and travel writer and the local correspondent for The Economist's online City Guide to San Francisco.

ACKNOWLEDGEMENTS

Manischewitz Moon by Peffy Landsman also appeared in Earth's Daughters and Poetica.

The Four Questions by Ellyn Maybe originally appeared in her self-published book Putting My 2 Cents In (1999).

The First Seder by Diana Sher originally appeared in Art Times, 2003

Blood, Frogs by Daniel A. Olivas first appeared in RealPoetik, April, 2001.

Ten Plagues by Daniel Y. Harris first appeared on PoetrySuperHighway.com in December of 2006.

A version of *Bitter* by Heather Mcnaugher originally appeared as "Seder" at PoetrySuperHighway.com in March, 2006.

Maror by Jonathan Penton also appears in his chapbook Prosthetic Gods. (Wing City Chapbooks)

After Dan Savage by Jonathan Penton also appears online at kagablog.com

Part III of David Gershator's Poem *Seder* originally appeared in the Book "Elijah's Child by David Gershator (Cross Cultural Communications, 1992)

Praise Small Things by Judith Pacht first appeared in Tebot Bach's 2001 Anthology.

Also a Full Moon by Helen Bar-Lev originally appeared online in Gostinaya Journal in December, 2007.

Hayei Olam by Jake Marmer first appeared online in The Blue Jew Yorker issue #2.

5744047R0

Made in the USA
Charleston, SC
28 July 2010